Happy as Larry

Written by Rachael Davis

Illustrated by Kelly Caswell

Collins

Four little friends knew each other so well.
Harry loved cooking, the taste and the smell,
While Carrie found reading and learning
    a blast,
And Ari loved anything daring and fast.

Larry loved nature and being outside.
Yet, still, there was one thing they
couldn't decide …

Carrie and Harry were happy like Ari,
But were they as happy as their buddy Larry?

Ari was smiling while wheeling and squealing,
Her tummy was filled with a warm fuzzy feeling.
"I know that we're happy," said Carrie to Ari,
"But how do we know we're as happy as Larry?"

"Perhaps, there's a way we can measure and test
Our happiness feeling, to see whose is best ..."
Ari agreed that it didn't seem fair–
    "Why's Larry so happy alone over there?"
"Enough," grumbled Harry. "I just want to be ..."

... as happy as Larry!

Me too!

And me three!

8

The threesome decided they needed more joy.
"Let's work out why Larry's the happiest boy."
So, Carrie devised them a cunning experiment.
"Tomorrow we'll watch him and copy
        his merriment!"

The trio knew Larry did art every morning. "Quick!" whispered Carrie. "There's NO time for yawning!"

They sat with their easels and painted the sky.
"I don't think art works," Ari said with a sigh.
"I'm not happy," said Harry, "with how my
     one looks."
And Carrie felt restless. "I'm missing my books."

The threesome observed Larry gobble his lunch,
And carefully copied him – every last munch!
Despite their best efforts and all of their might,
Their happiness dwindled with each bitter bite.

"Ugh," Ari moaned, "this tastes utterly YUCKY!"
And suddenly found herself feeling unlucky.
"It tastes fine to me," replied Harry, "but, wait,
I can't find the rest – is there no pudding plate?"

"We have to try harder," said Carrie aloud,
But all they could see was a looming
        grey cloud …
It started to pour. Larry danced in the rain.
The trio did nothing but moan and complain.

"Oh no, now it's thundering!" Ari was grumbling.
"No," Harry sighed, "it's my tummy
        that's rumbling."

15

Despite all their efforts, the threesome could see
That Larry was happier, jumping with glee!

"Enough!" Carrie cried. "I give up! I give in!
Just tell us, please, Larry, what gives you
          your grin?
We tried being you, but it made us feel worse.
Chasing your happiness felt like a curse!"

"I don't try to be happy, I try to be me.
I do what I love," Larry said, "I am free!
I'm not always happy. At times I feel sad,
But that's why I'm grateful each time
        I feel glad."

"Each day of the week, I note three joyful things,

Like painting ...

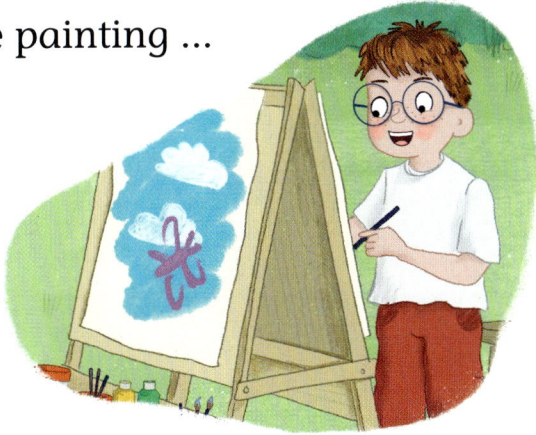

... and dancing

... and butterfly wings.

The happiest thing that has happened today ...

… is having the three of you ask me to play."

At last, Carrie saw what she'd missed
    all along …
"You can't compare happiness –
    trying was wrong.
There's something that all of us must keep
    in mind.
We should just be ourselves, have some fun
    and be kind.

Now Carrie was happy as Carrie,
And Harry was happy as Harry,
And Ari was happy as Ari,
And Larry was happy as Larry!

Happy as …

🐾 Ideas for reading 🐾

Written by Gill Matthews
Primary Literacy Consultant

Reading objectives:
- discussing and clarifying the meanings of words, linking new meanings to known vocabulary
- making inferences on the basis of what is being said and done
- answering and asking questions

Spoken language objectives:
- articulate and justify answers, arguments and opinions
- participate in discussions, presentations, performances, role play, improvisations and debates

Curriculum links: Relationships education: Caring friendships

Interest words: joy, merriment, glee, glad, joyful

Word count: 563

Build a context for reading

- Ask children to look at the front cover of the book and to read the title.
- Discuss with children what makes them happy and how they feel when they are happy.
- Read the back cover blurb. Explore what children think might happen in the story.

Understand and apply reading strategies

- Read pp2–9 aloud. Ask children what they notice about the story.
- Ask literal questions that involve children finding the answers in the text e.g. What does Harry love doing?
- Ask inferential questions that involve children reading between the lines e.g. Why do you think the children think Larry might be happier than them?
- Give children time to read the rest of the story, asking them to consider whether copying Larry makes the other characters happier.